I0422288

The Algorithmic Mind: Navigating IT Leadership in a Data-Driven World

Brian Beams

Printed in the United States of America

First Printing: March 2024

Visit my website for more key insights on IT Leadership and IT Transformation or to work with me

www.beamsfractionalcio.com

Table of Contents

Summary

In the era of big data and artificial intelligence, The Algorithmic Mind explores the role of IT leadership in harnessing the power of data. From predictive analytics to ethical considerations, it examines how IT leaders can leverage algorithms to drive innovation and make informed decisions.

Outline

I. Introduction

    A. Setting the Stage: The Rise of Big Data and AI
    B. The Evolving Role of IT Leadership
    C. Overview of the Book

II. Understanding Algorithms

    A. Defining Algorithms in the Context of IT Leadership
    B. Types of Algorithms and Their Applications
    C. The Power and Potential of Algorithmic Solutions

III. The Strategic Imperative

    A. Leveraging Algorithms for Business Strategy
    B. Identifying Opportunities for Algorithmic Innovation
    C. Balancing Short-term Wins with Long-term Vision

IV. Navigating Data Ethics

    A. Ethical Considerations in Algorithmic Decision-Making
    B. Ensuring Fairness, Accountability, and Transparency
    C. Mitigating Risks and Addressing Bias

V. Building a Data-Driven Culture

A. Cultivating Data Literacy Across the Organization
B. Fostering Collaboration Between IT and Business Units
C. Encouraging Experimentation and Learning from Data

VI. Leading Through Change

A. Overcoming Resistance to Algorithmic Adoption
B. Managing Cultural Shifts and Organizational Dynamics
C. Communicating the Value of Data-Driven Initiatives

VII. Case Studies and Practical Examples

A. Real-world Examples of Successful Algorithmic Implementations
B. Lessons Learned from Failures and Challenges
C. Practical Insights for IT Leaders

VIII. The Future of IT Leadership

A. Anticipating Trends in Data and AI
B. Adapting Leadership Practices to Technological Advancements
C. Continuing the Journey Towards Algorithmic Excellence

IX. Conclusion

A. Recap of Key Insights
B. Final Thoughts on Navigating IT Leadership in a Data-Driven World
C. Call to Action: Embracing the Algorithmic Mindset

Chapter Summaries

I. Introduction

    A. _Setting the Stage: The Rise of Big Data and AI_ - provides an overview of the current landscape, highlighting the increasing importance of big data and artificial intelligence in today's business environment.

    B. _The Evolving Role of IT Leadership_ - explores how the role of IT leadership has transformed in response to technological advancements, emphasizing the need for leaders to adapt to new challenges and opportunities.

    C. _Overview of the Book_ - gives readers a glimpse into what they can expect from the book, outlining the key themes and topics that will be covered in detail.

II. Understanding Algorithms

    A. Defining Algorithms in the Context of IT Leadership - delves into the concept of algorithms and their significance in the realm of IT leadership, laying the groundwork for understanding their role in decision-making and innovation.

    B. Types of Algorithms and Their Applications - explores the different types of algorithms commonly used in various industries and their practical applications, providing examples to illustrate their functionality.

C. The Power and Potential of Algorithmic Solutions - discusses the transformative potential of algorithmic solutions, highlighting their ability to drive efficiency, optimize processes, and uncover valuable insights from data.

III. The Strategic Imperative

A. _Leveraging Algorithms for Business Strategy_ - focuses on the strategic implications of leveraging algorithms in business decision-making, emphasizing their role in driving competitive advantage and achieving organizational goals.

B. Identifying Opportunities for Algorithmic Innovation - examines how IT leaders can identify and capitalize on opportunities for algorithmic innovation within their organizations, fostering a culture of experimentation and creativity.

C. _Balancing Short-term Wins with Long-term Vision_ - explores the importance of striking a balance between short-term wins and long-term strategic objectives when implementing algorithmic solutions, ensuring sustainable growth and success.

IV. Navigating Data Ethics

A. _Ethical Considerations in Algorithmic Decision-Making_ - addresses the ethical challenges associated with algorithmic decision-making, discussing issues such as bias, fairness, and accountability.

B. *Ensuring Fairness, Accountability, and Transparency* - examines strategies for promoting fairness, accountability, and transparency in algorithmic processes, mitigating potential risks, and fostering trust among stakeholders.

C. *Mitigating Risks and Addressing Bias* - offers practical guidance on how IT leaders can mitigate risks and address bias in algorithmic decision-making, implementing safeguards and protocols to ensure ethical outcomes.

V. Building a Data-Driven Culture

A. *Cultivating Data Literacy Across the Organization* - explores the importance of promoting data literacy across the organization, empowering employees to make informed decisions based on data-driven insights.

B. *Fostering Collaboration Between IT and Business Units* - discusses the need for collaboration between IT and business units in driving a data-driven culture, emphasizing the importance of aligning technological capabilities with strategic objectives.

C. *Encouraging Experimentation and Learning from Data* - encourages a culture of experimentation and continuous learning, highlighting the value of leveraging data to drive innovation and drive organizational growth.

VI. Leading Through Change

A. _Overcoming Resistance to Algorithmic Adoption_ - addresses common challenges and barriers to algorithmic adoption, providing strategies for overcoming resistance and driving organizational change.

B. _Managing Cultural Shifts and Organizational Dynamics_ - explores the cultural shifts and organizational dynamics that accompany algorithmic adoption, offering insights into effective change management strategies.

C. _Communicating the Value of Data-Driven Initiatives_ - discusses the importance of effective communication in promoting data-driven initiatives, highlighting strategies for articulating the value proposition and gaining buy-in from stakeholders.

VII. Case Studies and Practical Examples

A. _Real-world Examples of Successful Algorithmic Implementations_ - showcases real-world examples of successful algorithmic implementations, providing insights into best practices and lessons learned from industry leaders.

B. _Lessons Learned from Failures and Challenges_ - examines lessons learned from failures and challenges in algorithmic implementation, offering valuable insights into common pitfalls and how to avoid them.

C. *Practical Insights for IT Leaders* - offers practical insights and actionable takeaways for IT leaders looking to leverage algorithms effectively within their organizations, distilling key learnings from case studies and examples.

VIII. The Future of IT Leadership

A. *Anticipating Trends in Data and AI* - explores emerging trends in data and artificial intelligence, providing a glimpse into the future of IT leadership and the role of algorithms in driving innovation.

B. *Adapting Leadership Practices to Technological Advancements* - discusses how IT leaders can adapt their leadership practices to keep pace with technological advancements, ensuring they remain agile and responsive to change.

C. *Continuing the Journey Towards Algorithmic Excellence* - encourages a mindset of continuous improvement and learning, emphasizing the importance of ongoing development and refinement in the pursuit of algorithmic excellence.

IX. Conclusion

A. *Recap of Key Insights* - provides a recap of the key insights and takeaways from the book, reinforcing the importance of embracing the algorithmic mindset in IT leadership.

11

B. _Final Thoughts on Navigating IT Leadership in a Data-Driven World_ - offers final reflections on navigating IT leadership in a data-driven world, highlighting the opportunities and challenges that lie ahead.

C. _Call to Action: Embracing the Algorithmic Mindset_ - concludes with a call to action for readers to embrace the algorithmic mindset and take proactive steps towards leveraging algorithms effectively within their organizations.

Chapter I: Introduction

In the evolving landscape of technology, where data flows like a digital river and artificial intelligence breathes life into complex algorithms, the role of IT leadership has become pivotal. As we stand on the precipice of a new era, marked by the convergence of big data and artificial intelligence, the need for adept leaders who can navigate the intricacies of this dynamic landscape has never been more pronounced.

A. Setting the Stage: The Rise of Big Data and AI

Imagine a world where every interaction, transaction, and engagement leaves a digital footprint – a world where the sheer volume of data generated daily is astronomical. Welcome to the era of big data. The rise of digital technologies, coupled with the interconnectedness of our lives, has given birth to an unprecedented era of data abundance. From social media interactions and online purchases to sensor data from the Internet of Things (IoT), every click, swipe, and sensor reading contributes to the vast ocean of information known as big data.

It is within this sea of data that artificial intelligence (AI) emerges as a transformative force. AI, with its ability to analyze massive datasets, identify patterns, and make intelligent predictions, has become the engine that propels innovation across industries. From predictive analytics that foresee market trends to machine learning algorithms that enhance decision-making, AI has become the driving force behind digital transformation.

The rise of big data and artificial intelligence (AI) marks a paradigm shift of monumental proportions. Gone are the days when organizations merely collected data for record-keeping purposes. Today, data has become a strategic asset, a source of competitive advantage, and a catalyst for innovation.

1. Harnessing the Power of Data:

Big data represents a seismic shift in the way organizations collect, process, and utilize information. With the proliferation of digital technologies and the interconnectedness of our lives, the volume, velocity, and variety of data being generated have reached unprecedented levels. From customer interactions and online transactions to sensor data from IoT devices, every click, swipe, and sensor reading contributes to the vast ocean of information known as big data.

2. Transformative Potential of AI:

Accompanying the rise of big data is the emergence of artificial intelligence – the engine that powers insights and innovation from vast datasets. AI technologies, such as machine learning and natural language processing, can analyze massive amounts of data, identify patterns, and make intelligent predictions. From predictive analytics that forecast market trends to chatbots that enhance customer service, AI has become a game-changer across industries.

3. Redefining IT Leadership:

In this landscape of big data and AI, the role of IT leadership is undergoing a profound transformation. No longer confined to the back rooms of server management, IT leaders are now at the forefront of strategic decision-making, influencing the direction of entire organizations. The essence of IT leadership is shifting from a focus on technology management to a focus on leveraging data and AI to drive innovation, optimize processes, and gain a competitive edge.

4. Real-world Implications:

The implications of big data and AI are far-reaching and profound, reshaping the business landscape in fundamental ways. Organizations that harness the power of data and AI can gain deeper insights into customer behavior, streamline operations, and create personalized experiences that drive loyalty and satisfaction. Conversely, those who fail to adapt risk falling behind, unable to keep pace with the demands of the digital age.

5. Leadership in the Information Technology Domain:

In this era of big data and AI, leadership in the Information Technology domain is no longer just about managing technology infrastructure. It's about harnessing the power of data and AI to drive strategic initiatives, foster innovation, and achieve organizational goals. IT leaders must possess a deep understanding of both technology and business, navigating the complexities of data governance, ethical considerations, and organizational dynamics with skill and foresight.

The rise of big data and AI represents a paradigm shift of unprecedented magnitude, where organizations are no longer merely collecting data but harnessing its power to gain a competitive edge. In this new era, leadership in the Information Technology domain is defined by the ability to leverage data and AI to drive innovation and shape the future of organizations.

B. The Evolving Role of IT Leadership

As technology accelerates at an unprecedented pace, the role of IT leadership is undergoing a profound transformation. Gone are the days when IT leaders were confined to the back rooms, managing servers, and troubleshooting technical glitches. Today, IT leaders are at the forefront of strategic decision-making, influencing the direction of entire organizations.

The evolution of IT leadership is not merely a response to the advancements in technology but a proactive adaptation to the changing needs of businesses. We will explore how IT leaders have transcended their traditional roles to become architects of digital strategies, innovators who leverage technology for competitive advantage, and guardians of data integrity and security. The challenges faced by IT leaders are multifaceted – from managing complex technological ecosystems to aligning IT initiatives with overarching business objectives. This evolution can be understood through several layers:

1. **Strategic Visionaries:** IT leaders have transitioned from being mere implementers of technology to strategic visionaries who shape the direction of the organization. With a deep understanding of both technology and business, they can identify opportunities for leveraging data and AI to drive innovation and gain a competitive edge.

2. **Change Agents:** In the face of rapid technological advancement, IT leaders have become change agents within their organizations. They play a pivotal role in driving digital transformation initiatives, fostering a culture of innovation, and

leading organizational change efforts to adapt to the demands of the digital age.

3. Data Stewards: As custodians of data, IT leaders are responsible for ensuring the integrity, security, and accessibility of organizational data assets. They oversee data governance processes, establish data management policies, and implement robust security measures to protect sensitive information.

4. Collaborative Partners: IT leaders must collaborate closely with business units and other stakeholders to align technological capabilities with strategic objectives. By fostering cross-functional collaboration and communication, they ensure that technology initiatives are closely aligned with the needs and priorities of the organization.

Skills and Mindset Required:

Thriving in this fast-paced evolving environment requires a unique set of skills and mindset:

1. Continuous Learning: IT leaders must possess a thirst for knowledge and a commitment to lifelong learning. They must stay abreast of emerging technologies, industry trends, and best practices, continuously expanding their skills to stay ahead of the curve.

2. Adaptability: In a world of rapid technological change, adaptability is key. IT leaders must be able to quickly pivot and respond to changing circumstances, embracing new technologies and methodologies to drive innovation and achieve organizational goals.

3. Visionary Thinking: To navigate the complexities of the data-driven world, IT leaders must possess a visionary mindset. They must be able to anticipate future trends, identify emerging opportunities, and chart a course for the organization that ensures long-term success.

4. Collaboration and Communication: Effective collaboration and communication skills are essential for IT leaders. They must be able to build strong relationships with stakeholders, facilitate cross-functional teamwork, and articulate complex technical concepts in a way that is easily understood by non-technical audiences.

The evolving role of IT leadership in the data-driven world demands a unique blend of strategic vision, technical expertise, and interpersonal skills. By embracing continuous learning, adaptability, and visionary thinking, IT leaders can thrive in this fast-paced environment and drive organizational success in the digital age.

C. Overview of the Book

As we embark on this exploration of the algorithmic mind and its role in IT leadership, it is crucial to provide a roadmap for our journey. This section serves as a compass, guiding readers through the key themes and topics that will be dissected and discussed in the pages that follow.

The Algorithmic Mind: Navigating IT Leadership in a Data-Driven World is not merely a theoretical discourse. It is a practical guide for IT leaders, executives, and aspiring tech professionals seeking to understand and harness the power of algorithms. Throughout the book, we will delve into the nuances of algorithmic decision-making, the strategic imperatives of leveraging algorithms for business success, and the ethical considerations that accompany this transformative journey.

Readers can expect to gain insights into building a data-driven culture within their organizations, overcoming challenges in algorithmic adoption, and envisioning the future of IT leadership in an era dominated by data and artificial intelligence. Each chapter is designed to provide tangible takeaways, blending theoretical knowledge with real-world examples and actionable strategies.

So, fasten your seatbelts as we embark on a journey into the heart of the algorithmic mind, where data meets innovation, and IT leadership emerges as the guiding force in this data-driven world.

Chapter II: Understanding Algorithms

In the realm of IT leadership, algorithms serve as the building blocks of innovation, driving decision-making and shaping strategic initiatives. In this chapter, we will embark on a journey to unravel the intricacies of algorithms, exploring their significance, types, and transformative potential within the context of IT leadership.

A. Defining Algorithms in the Context of IT Leadership

At its core, an algorithm is a step-by-step procedure or set of rules designed to solve a particular problem or perform a specific task. In the context of IT leadership, algorithms serve as the computational engines that power data-driven decision-making and drive organizational innovation.

Understanding algorithms is essential for IT leaders, as they are tasked with harnessing the power of data to drive strategic initiatives and achieve business objectives. Whether it's optimizing supply chain operations, personalizing customer experiences, or predicting market trends, algorithms play a central role in driving efficiency, effectiveness, and competitiveness.

Role in the Decision-Making Process:

Algorithms serve as powerful tools for IT leaders, enabling them to make data-driven decisions with speed and precision. By leveraging algorithms, IT leaders can analyze complex datasets, identify trends and patterns, and generate actionable insights that inform strategic initiatives and drive organizational success.

In the decision-making process, algorithms can be used to:

- Predict future trends and outcomes based on historical data.
- Identify opportunities for optimization and efficiency improvements.
- Automate routine tasks and processes, freeing up time for strategic activities.
- Personalize customer experiences and tailor offerings to individual preferences.
- Mitigate risks and identify potential threats to the organization.

Significance in Driving Innovation:

Algorithms are also instrumental in driving innovation within organizations. By harnessing the power of data and AI, IT leaders can uncover new opportunities, solve complex problems, and create value for stakeholders. Whether it's developing new products and services, optimizing business processes, or enhancing customer experiences, algorithms provide a foundation for innovation and growth.

Innovation driven by algorithms can lead to:

- New revenue streams and business models.
- Improved operational efficiency and cost savings.
- Enhanced customer satisfaction and loyalty.
- Competitive differentiation in the marketplace.
- Increased agility and responsiveness to changing market conditions.

Leveraging Algorithms for Organizational Success:

To better leverage algorithms and drive organizational success, IT leaders must first understand the capabilities and limitations of these powerful tools. This requires a deep understanding of data science principles, statistical analysis techniques, and machine learning algorithms.

IT leaders can also benefit from:

- Investing in data infrastructure and technology platforms that enable efficient data processing and analysis.
- Building cross-functional teams with diverse skill sets, including data scientists, analysts, and domain experts.
- Establishing clear goals and objectives for algorithmic initiatives, with a focus on delivering tangible business value.
- Embracing a culture of experimentation and learning, where failure is viewed as an opportunity for growth and innovation.
- Ensuring that algorithmic decision-making processes are transparent, accountable, and aligned with ethical principles.

Algorithms play a central role in IT leadership, driving decision-making processes and fueling innovation within organizations. By understanding the significance of algorithms and leveraging them effectively, IT leaders can unlock new opportunities, solve complex problems, and drive organizational success.

B. Types of Algorithms and Their Applications

Algorithms come in various types, each designed to address specific types of problems and tasks. In this section, we'll explore different types of algorithms and their practical applications across industries, highlighting real-world examples to illustrate their capabilities and limitations. Additionally, we'll discuss how IT leaders can make informed decisions about which algorithms to deploy and how to optimize their performance within their business.

1. Machine Learning Algorithms: Machine learning algorithms, for example, are designed to learn from data and make predictions or decisions without being explicitly programmed. And is a the heart of many types of other algorithms, such as:

- Image Recognition/Computer Vision: Identifying objects, faces, or activities in images or videos.

    - *Example*: Autonomous vehicles use computer vision algorithms to recognize traffic signs, pedestrians, and other vehicles on the road to make driving decisions.

- Natural Language Processing (NLP): Processing and understanding human language data.

    - *Example*: Chatbots like Siri or Alexa utilize NLP algorithms to understand and respond to user queries in natural language.

- Recommendation Systems: Suggesting products, movies, or content based on user preferences and behavior.

- o *Example*: Netflix uses recommendation algorithms to suggest movies or TV shows to users based on their viewing history and preferences.

- Predictive Analytics: Forecasting future trends or outcomes based on historical data.

  - o *Example*: Financial institutions use predictive analytics to forecast stock prices or detect fraudulent transactions based on patterns in past data.

- Healthcare Diagnostics: Assisting in medical diagnosis and decision-making.

  - o *Example*: Machine learning models are used in medical imaging to detect abnormalities in X-rays, MRIs, or CT scans, aiding radiologists in diagnosing diseases like cancer.

- Fraud Detection: Identifying fraudulent activities or transactions.

  - o *Example*: Credit card companies use machine learning algorithms to analyze patterns in transaction data and flag suspicious activities, such as unusual spending patterns or transactions from unfamiliar locations.

- Sentiment Analysis: Analyzing and understanding opinions, attitudes, and emotions expressed in text data.

  - o *Example*: Social media platforms use sentiment analysis to gauge public opinion on various topics by analyzing user comments and posts.

25

- Autonomous Vehicles: Navigating and operating vehicles without human intervention.

  - *Example*: Companies like Tesla and Waymo employ machine learning algorithms to enable self-driving cars to perceive their environment, make decisions, and navigate safely on roads.

2. Optimization Algorithms: Optimization algorithms, on the other hand, are used to find the best solution to a problem from a set of possible solutions. These algorithms are commonly used in logistics, scheduling, and resource allocation, helping organizations optimize their operations and maximize efficiency.

- Logistics Optimization: Finding the most efficient routes for transportation, minimizing costs and delivery times.

  - *Example*: Companies like UPS or FedEx use optimization algorithms to optimize their delivery routes, considering factors such as package weight, vehicle capacity, traffic conditions, and delivery deadlines.

- Scheduling Optimization: Scheduling tasks, appointments, or workforce shifts to maximize productivity and minimize idle time.

  - *Example*: Hospitals use optimization algorithms to schedule surgeries, allocate staff resources, and manage patient appointments, ensuring efficient use of medical resources and reducing wait times for patients.

- Supply Chain Management: Optimizing inventory levels, production schedules, and distribution networks to meet demand while minimizing costs.

  - *Example*: Retail companies employ optimization algorithms to optimize inventory replenishment, determine optimal warehouse locations, and plan transportation routes to ensure timely delivery of goods while minimizing holding costs.

- Resource Allocation: Allocating resources such as manpower, equipment, or funds to various projects or tasks to maximize overall performance.

  - *Example*: Project management teams use optimization algorithms to allocate human resources, budget allocations, and equipment usage across different projects to maximize project completion rates within given constraints.

- Portfolio Optimization: Selecting the optimal mix of financial assets to achieve desired returns while managing risk.

  - *Example*: Investment firms use optimization algorithms to construct investment portfolios that maximize returns while minimizing risk, considering factors such as asset correlations, expected returns, and investment constraints.

- Energy Optimization: Optimizing energy consumption in buildings, industrial processes, or transportation systems to reduce costs and environmental impact.

- *Example*: Smart grid systems use optimization algorithms to manage energy distribution and consumption, optimizing the use of renewable energy sources, storage systems, and demand-response programs to minimize energy waste and reduce carbon emissions.

- Production Planning: Planning production schedules, inventory levels, and resource utilization in manufacturing processes.

    - *Example*: Manufacturing companies use optimization algorithms to optimize production schedules, minimize production costs, and ensure timely delivery of products to meet customer demand while maximizing profit margins.

3. Classification Algorithms: Classification algorithms are used to categorize data into predefined classes or categories. They are commonly used in applications such as:

- Spam detection: Classifying emails as either spam or non-spam.
- Customer segmentation: Identifying groups of customers based on demographic or behavioral attributes.
- Disease diagnosis: Classifying medical images or patient data to diagnose diseases.

Example: In the healthcare industry, classification algorithms are used to analyze medical images such as X-rays and MRI scans to classify them as either normal or indicative of a specific condition, such as cancer or fractures.

4. Regression Algorithms: Regression algorithms are used to predict continuous numerical values based on input features. They are commonly used in applications such as:

- Sales forecasting: Predicting future sales based on historical data and market trends.
- Stock price prediction: Forecasting the future price of stocks based on historical trading data.
- Demand forecasting: Estimating future demand for products or services based on past sales data.

Example: In the retail industry, regression algorithms are used to analyze historical sales data and predict future demand for products, enabling retailers to optimize inventory levels and minimize stockouts.

5. Clustering Algorithms: Clustering algorithms are used to group similar data points based on their characteristics. They are commonly used in applications such as:

- Market segmentation: Identifying groups of customers with similar purchasing behavior.
- Image segmentation: Grouping pixels in an image based on their color or intensity.
- Anomaly detection: Identifying unusual patterns or outliers in data.

Example: In the e-commerce industry, clustering algorithms are used to segment customers into different groups based on their browsing and purchasing behavior, allowing retailers to personalize marketing campaigns and recommend relevant products to each customer segment.

6. Recommendation Algorithms: Recommendation algorithms are used to provide personalized recommendations to users based on their preferences and behavior. They are commonly used in applications such as:

- E-commerce product recommendations: Suggesting products to users based on their past purchases and browsing history.
- Content recommendations: Recommending articles, videos, or music based on user preferences.
- Movie or TV show recommendations: Suggesting movies or TV shows to users based on their viewing history and ratings.

Example: In the entertainment industry, recommendation algorithms are used by streaming platforms like Netflix and Spotify to analyze user behavior and recommend personalized content, leading to increased user engagement and satisfaction.

Making Informed Decisions and Optimization:

When deciding which algorithms to deploy, IT leaders must consider factors such as the nature of the problem, the available data, and the desired outcomes. It's essential to assess the strengths and limitations of each algorithm and choose the one that best fits the specific requirements of the task at hand.

To optimize the performance of algorithms within their business, IT leaders can:

- Experiment with different algorithms and parameter settings to find the optimal configuration.
- Continuously monitor and evaluate the performance of algorithms and adjust as needed.

- Invest in data quality and preprocessing techniques to ensure that input data is clean, relevant, and representative.
- Collaborate with data scientists and domain experts to gain insights into the underlying data and refine the algorithmic models accordingly.

By making informed decisions about algorithm selection and optimization, IT leaders can harness the power of algorithms to drive innovation, improve decision-making, and achieve business objectives across industries.

C. The Power and Potential of Algorithmic Solutions

The transformative potential of algorithmic solutions cannot be overstated. From driving efficiency and optimizing processes to uncovering valuable insights from data, algorithms hold the key to unlocking new opportunities and driving innovation within organizations.

Algorithmic solutions have emerged as powerful tools that have the potential to revolutionize how organizations operate and compete. From streamlining operations to enhancing customer experiences and identifying new revenue streams, algorithms have the power to drive organizational performance and gain a competitive advantage.

1. Streamlining Operations:

One of the key benefits of algorithmic solutions is their ability to streamline operations and optimize business processes. By automating routine tasks, analyzing data to identify inefficiencies, and providing real-time insights, algorithms enable organizations to operate more efficiently and effectively.

31

For example, algorithms can be used in supply chain management to optimize inventory levels, minimize stockouts, and reduce transportation costs. They can also be used in manufacturing to improve production scheduling, reduce downtime, and increase overall productivity.

2. Enhancing Customer Experiences:

Algorithms play a crucial role in enhancing customer experiences by providing personalized and relevant interactions at every touchpoint. By analyzing customer data, preferences, and behavior, algorithms enable organizations to deliver targeted marketing messages, recommend products or services, and tailor offerings to individual needs.

For example, recommendation algorithms used by e-commerce platforms can analyze past purchase history and browsing behavior to suggest relevant products to customers, increasing conversion rates and driving revenue. Similarly, algorithms used in customer service chatbots can analyze customer inquiries and provide timely and accurate responses, improving overall satisfaction and loyalty.

3. Identifying New Revenue Streams:

Algorithmic solutions have the potential to identify new revenue streams and business opportunities by analyzing data and uncovering insights that may not be apparent through traditional methods. By identifying emerging trends, market opportunities, and customer needs, algorithms enable organizations to innovate and create value in new and unexpected ways.

For example, algorithms can be used in predictive analytics to forecast future market trends and consumer behavior, enabling organizations to proactively respond to changing market conditions and capitalize on emerging opportunities. Similarly, algorithms used in data monetization strategies can analyze customer data to identify new products or services that may appeal to specific market segments, driving revenue growth and market expansion.

Key Takeaways

The power and potential of algorithmic solutions are vast and transformative. From streamlining operations to enhancing customer experiences and identifying new revenue streams, algorithms have the ability to revolutionize how organizations operate and compete in today's digital age. By leveraging the power of algorithms, organizations can drive organizational performance, gain a competitive advantage, and position themselves for long-term success in an increasingly data-driven world.

Chapter III: The Strategic Imperative

Strategic decision-making is paramount for organizational success. In this chapter, we will explore the strategic imperative of leveraging algorithms within the context of IT leadership, examining how these powerful tools can drive competitive advantage, foster innovation, and propel organizations toward their long-term goals.

A. Leveraging Algorithms for Business Strategy

At the heart of every successful business strategy lies data-driven decision-making. Algorithms play a crucial role in this process, providing organizations with the insights they need to identify opportunities, mitigate risks, and optimize their performance.

Leveraging algorithms has become increasingly essential for organizations seeking to gain a competitive advantage and achieve their organizational goals. Algorithms play a crucial role in driving informed decision-making, optimizing processes, and capitalizing on market opportunities. In this section, we'll outline the strategic implications of leveraging algorithms in business decision-making, emphasizing their role in driving competitive advantage and achieving organizational goals.

1. Identifying Market Trends and Predicting Consumer Behavior:

Algorithms enable organizations to analyze vast amounts of data and identify market trends and patterns that may not be apparent through traditional methods. By leveraging predictive analytics algorithms, organizations can forecast future market trends, anticipate changes in consumer behavior, and proactively respond to emerging opportunities or threats. This strategic foresight allows organizations to stay ahead of the competition and capitalize on market shifts to drive sustainable growth.

2. Optimizing Resource Allocation:

Effective resource allocation is essential for organizations to maximize efficiency and achieve their strategic objectives. Algorithms can help organizations optimize resource allocation by analyzing data and identifying areas where resources can be allocated most effectively. Whether it's optimizing inventory levels, allocating marketing budgets, or scheduling workforce resources, algorithms enable organizations to make data-driven decisions that maximize ROI and drive operational excellence.

3. Streamlining Operations:

Algorithms play a critical role in streamlining operations and optimizing business processes to improve efficiency and reduce costs. By automating routine tasks, analyzing data to identify bottlenecks or inefficiencies, and providing real-time insights, algorithms enable organizations to streamline operations and enhance productivity. This strategic focus on operational excellence allows organizations to deliver products and services more efficiently, reduce time-to-market, and gain a competitive edge in the marketplace.

4. Personalizing Customer Experiences:

In today's hyper-connected world, delivering personalized customer experiences is essential for organizations to drive customer loyalty and retention. Algorithms enable organizations to analyze customer data, preferences, and behavior to deliver targeted marketing messages, personalized product recommendations, and tailored customer service interactions. This strategic focus on customer personalization allows organizations to build stronger relationships with customers, increase customer satisfaction, and drive long-term loyalty and advocacy.

Leveraging algorithms for business strategy has become indispensable for organizations seeking to gain a competitive advantage and achieve their organizational goals. From identifying market trends and predicting consumer behavior to optimizing resource allocation and streamlining operations, algorithms empower organizations to make informed decisions that drive sustainable growth and success. By strategically leveraging algorithms, organizations can unlock new opportunities, optimize performance, and position themselves for long-term success in an increasingly competitive marketplace.

B. Identifying Opportunities for Algorithmic Innovation

Innovation is the lifeblood of every organization, driving growth, and differentiation in an increasingly competitive marketplace. Algorithms provide a fertile ground for innovation, enabling organizations to uncover new opportunities, solve complex problems, and create value for their stakeholders.

Identifying and capitalizing on opportunities for algorithmic innovation is essential for organizations seeking to maintain a competitive edge and drive business success. IT leaders play a pivotal role in fostering a culture of experimentation and creativity, empowering their teams to explore new ideas, test hypotheses, and develop innovative solutions. In this section, we'll explore how IT leaders can identify and capitalize on opportunities for algorithmic innovation within their organizations.

1. Stay Abreast of Technological Trends:

To identify opportunities for algorithmic innovation, IT leaders must stay abreast of technological trends and advancements in the fields of data science, artificial intelligence, and machine learning. By continuously monitoring industry developments, attending conferences, and networking with experts, IT leaders can gain insights into emerging technologies and potential applications within their organizations.

2. Engage with Stakeholders:

Effective communication and collaboration with stakeholders are essential for identifying opportunities for algorithmic innovation. IT leaders should engage with key stakeholders across departments to understand their pain points, challenges, and strategic objectives. By soliciting input from business units, marketing teams, and operations staff, IT leaders can identify areas where algorithmic solutions can add value and drive business impact.

3. Foster a Culture of Experimentation:

A culture of experimentation is critical for fostering algorithmic innovation within organizations. IT leaders should create an environment where team members feel empowered to explore new ideas, test hypotheses, and take calculated risks. By encouraging curiosity, creativity, and open-mindedness, IT leaders can inspire their teams to push the boundaries of what is possible and develop innovative solutions that drive business success.

4. Provide Resources and Support:

IT leaders must provide the necessary resources and support to enable algorithmic innovation within their organizations. This may include investing in training and development programs to build team members' skills in data science and machine learning, providing access to cutting-edge tools and technologies, and creating cross-functional teams to tackle complex problems collaboratively. By providing the right resources and support, IT leaders can empower their teams to innovate and drive meaningful change within the organization.

5. Encourage Knowledge Sharing and Collaboration:

Knowledge sharing and collaboration are essential for driving algorithmic innovation within organizations. IT leaders should encourage team members to share their expertise, insights, and best practices with one another, fostering a culture of collaboration and collective learning. By facilitating cross-functional collaboration and creating opportunities for knowledge exchange, IT leaders can harness the collective intelligence of their teams to identify new opportunities for algorithmic innovation and develop innovative solutions that drive business success.

Identifying and capitalizing on opportunities for algorithmic innovation requires proactive leadership, effective communication, and a culture of experimentation and collaboration. By staying abreast of technological trends, engaging with stakeholders, fostering a culture of experimentation, providing resources and support, and encouraging knowledge sharing and collaboration, IT leaders can empower their teams to explore new ideas, develop innovative solutions, and drive business success through algorithmic innovation.

C. Balancing Short-term Wins with Long-term Vision

In the pursuit of organizational success, striking a balance between short-term wins and long-term strategic objectives is essential. While algorithms offer the promise of immediate gains and efficiencies, organizations must maintain a focus on their long-term vision and objectives.

In the world of technology, IT leaders often face the challenge of balancing short-term wins with long-term strategic objectives when implementing algorithmic solutions within their organizations. While short-term wins can provide immediate benefits and drive momentum, focusing solely on short-term gains can lead to missed opportunities and hinder long-term success.

In this section, we'll explore the importance of striking this balance and how IT leaders can ensure sustainable growth and success by aligning short-term wins with long-term vision.

1. Avoiding Short-Sighted Decision-Making:

One of the key pitfalls of focusing solely on short-term wins is the risk of short-sighted decision-making. When organizations prioritize immediate gains over long-term strategic objectives, they may overlook potential risks, trade-offs, and unintended consequences of their actions. This can lead to suboptimal outcomes and hinder the organization's ability to achieve its long-term goals.

2. Maintaining Focus on the Bigger Picture:

By balancing short-term wins with long-term vision, IT leaders can ensure that their organizations maintain focus on the bigger picture and stay aligned with their long-term strategic objectives. This requires taking a holistic approach to decision-making, considering the potential long-term implications of short-term actions, and prioritizing initiatives that support the organization's overarching goals and values.

4. Building Sustainable Solutions:

Short-term wins often involve quick fixes or temporary solutions that address immediate challenges but may not be sustainable in the long run. By contrast, focusing on long-term strategic objectives allows organizations to build sustainable solutions that provide lasting value and resilience. This may involve investing in infrastructure, talent development, and process improvements that lay the foundation for future growth and innovation.

4. Navigating Trade-Offs and Risks:

Balancing short-term wins with long-term vision requires IT leaders to navigate trade-offs and risks effectively. This may involve making difficult decisions about resource allocation, prioritization, and risk management, weighing the potential short-term benefits against the long-term impact on the organization's goals and objectives. By taking a strategic approach to decision-making and considering the broader implications of their actions, IT leaders can mitigate risks and optimize outcomes for sustainable growth and success.

5. Embracing Agility and Adaptability:

In today's rapidly changing business environment, agility and adaptability are essential for success. IT leaders must be prepared to pivot and adjust their strategies in response to evolving market conditions, technological advancements, and competitive pressures. By balancing short-term wins with long-term vision, IT leaders can foster a culture of agility and adaptability within their organizations, enabling them to respond effectively to change and seize new opportunities for growth and innovation.

Key Takeaways

Striking a balance between short-term wins and long-term vision is essential for ensuring sustainable growth and success when implementing algorithmic solutions within organizations. By avoiding short-sighted decision-making, maintaining focus on the bigger picture, building sustainable solutions, navigating trade-offs and risks effectively, and embracing agility and adaptability, IT leaders can align short-term wins with long-term strategic objectives and drive meaningful impact for their organizations.

By harnessing the power of algorithms to drive strategic decision-making, foster innovation, and achieve organizational goals, IT leaders can position their organizations for success in an increasingly competitive and data-driven world.

Chapter IV: Navigating Data Ethics

In the age of big data and artificial intelligence, the ethical implications of algorithmic decision-making loom large. As IT leaders navigate the complex landscape of data-driven innovation, it is imperative to prioritize ethical considerations to ensure that algorithms are used responsibly and ethically. In this chapter, we will explore the ethical challenges associated with algorithmic decision-making and discuss strategies for promoting fairness, accountability, and transparency.

A. Ethical Considerations in Algorithmic Decision-Making

Algorithmic decision-making raises a host of ethical concerns, ranging from issues of bias and fairness to questions of accountability and transparency. As algorithms increasingly influence important aspects of our lives, from healthcare and finance to employment and education, it is essential to address these ethical challenges head-on.

In the era of algorithmic decision-making, IT leaders must grapple with a myriad of ethical considerations to ensure that their organizations operate responsibly and uphold the rights and well-being of all stakeholders. From addressing bias and discrimination to protecting privacy and autonomy, ethical considerations play a crucial role in guiding the deployment of algorithmic solutions within organizations. In this section, we'll outline and explain in detail the ethical considerations that IT leaders must navigate when deploying algorithmic solutions.

1. Bias and Discrimination:

One of the most pressing ethical considerations in algorithmic decision-making is the risk of bias and discrimination. Algorithms rely on historical data to make predictions and recommendations, and if this data is biased or reflects existing inequalities, it can perpetuate and exacerbate bias and discrimination in decision-making processes. IT leaders must ensure that algorithms are trained on unbiased data and are designed to mitigate the risk of bias and discrimination in their outputs.

2. Transparency and Accountability:

Transparency and accountability are essential for building trust and ensuring accountability in algorithmic decision-making. IT leaders must ensure that algorithmic processes are transparent and explainable, enabling stakeholders to understand how decisions are made and assess the fairness and reliability of algorithmic outputs. Additionally, IT leaders must establish mechanisms for accountability, ensuring that decision-makers are held responsible for the outcomes of algorithmic decisions.

3. Privacy and Autonomy:

Protecting the privacy and autonomy of individuals is paramount in algorithmic decision-making. Algorithms often rely on vast amounts of personal data to make predictions and recommendations, raising concerns about data privacy and consent. IT leaders must ensure that algorithms comply with privacy regulations and best practices for data protection and that individuals are informed about how their data is used and have the ability to exercise control over their personal information.

4. Fairness and Equity:

Ensuring fairness and equity in algorithmic decision-making is essential for promoting social justice and equality. Algorithms must be designed to treat all individuals fairly and impartially, regardless of race, gender, ethnicity, or other protected characteristics. IT leaders must carefully evaluate the potential impact of algorithmic decisions on different demographic groups and take steps to mitigate any disparities or inequalities that may arise.

5. Human Oversight and Intervention:

While algorithms can automate many decision-making processes, human oversight and intervention are essential to ensure ethical decision-making and safeguard against unintended consequences. IT leaders must establish processes for human oversight and intervention, enabling human decision-makers to review and override algorithmic recommendations, when necessary, particularly in cases where the stakes are high or the outcomes are uncertain.

Ethical considerations play a crucial role in guiding the deployment of algorithmic solutions within organizations. IT leaders must grapple with complex ethical dilemmas related to bias and discrimination, transparency and accountability, privacy and autonomy, fairness and equity, and human oversight and intervention. By upholding ethical standards and prioritizing the rights and well-being of all stakeholders, IT leaders can ensure that algorithmic decision-making processes are responsible, fair, and aligned with organizational values and objectives.

B. Ensuring Fairness, Accountability, and Transparency

Promoting fairness, accountability, and transparency in algorithmic processes is essential to building trust and credibility among stakeholders. In the realm of data ethics, ensuring fairness, accountability, and transparency is paramount for building trust, mitigating risks, and upholding the rights of individuals and communities. IT leaders must implement strategies that promote fairness, establish clear lines of accountability, and foster transparency in algorithmic decision-making processes. In this section, we'll outline strategies for achieving these goals, including the use of fairness metrics and algorithms, establishing clear lines of accountability, and implementing transparent decision-making processes.

1. Use of Fairness Metrics and Algorithms:

To ensure fairness in algorithmic decision-making, IT leaders must utilize fairness metrics and algorithms that assess and mitigate bias and discrimination. Fairness metrics measure the impact of algorithmic decisions on different demographic groups and identify disparities or inequalities in outcomes. Fairness algorithms adjust the decision-making process to mitigate bias and ensure equitable outcomes for all stakeholders. IT leaders must prioritize the development and implementation of fairness metrics and algorithms to promote fairness in algorithmic decision-making processes.

2. Establishing Clear Lines of Accountability:

Accountability is essential for ensuring that decision-makers are held responsible for the outcomes of algorithmic decisions. IT leaders must establish clear lines of accountability within their organizations, defining roles and responsibilities for individuals involved in algorithmic decision-making processes. This includes identifying decision-makers, data scientists, and other stakeholders responsible for designing, implementing, and monitoring algorithms. By establishing clear lines of accountability, IT leaders can ensure that decision-makers are held accountable for the ethical implications of algorithmic decisions.

3. Implementing Transparent Decision-Making Processes:

Transparency is crucial for building trust and enabling stakeholders to understand how algorithmic decisions are made. IT leaders must implement transparent decision-making processes that provide visibility into the inputs, methodologies, and outcomes of algorithmic systems. This includes documenting data sources, pre-processing techniques, model architectures, and decision criteria used in algorithmic decision-making. Additionally, IT leaders must communicate openly with stakeholders about the rationale behind algorithmic decisions and provide mechanisms for feedback. By implementing transparent decision-making processes, IT leaders can enhance trust, accountability, and legitimacy in algorithmic decision-making.

4. Auditing and Monitoring:

Regular auditing and monitoring of algorithmic systems are essential for identifying and addressing potential biases, errors, or unintended consequences. IT leaders must establish processes for auditing and monitoring algorithmic systems, including regular assessments of fairness, accuracy, and reliability. Auditing involves examining the inputs, outputs, and decision-making processes of algorithms to identify biases or inconsistencies. Monitoring involves ongoing surveillance of algorithmic systems to detect deviations from expected behavior or performance. By conducting regular audits and monitoring, IT leaders can identify and address issues in algorithmic systems before they escalate into larger problems.

Ensuring fairness, accountability, and transparency in algorithmic decision-making is essential for building trust, promoting social justice, and upholding ethical standards. IT leaders must implement strategies that promote fairness, establish clear lines of accountability, and foster transparency in algorithmic decision-making processes.

By utilizing fairness metrics and algorithms, establishing clear lines of accountability, implementing transparent decision-making processes, and conducting regular audits and monitoring, IT leaders can ensure that algorithmic decision-making processes are responsible, fair, and aligned with organizational values and by promoting fairness, accountability, and transparency in algorithmic processes, IT leaders can mitigate potential risks and foster trust among stakeholders. Whether it's through the use of explainable AI techniques or the establishment of oversight mechanisms, there are various strategies that organizations can employ to ensure that their algorithmic decision-making processes are ethical and responsible.

C. Mitigating Risks and Addressing Bias

One of the most significant challenges in algorithmic decision-making is the risk of bias and discrimination. Biases can creep into algorithms at various stages of the development process, from data collection and preprocessing to algorithm design and implementation. Left unchecked, these biases can perpetuate existing inequalities and lead to unfair or discriminatory outcomes.

Mitigating risks and addressing bias is crucial for organizations to ensure fairness, transparency, and ethical integrity. IT leaders play a pivotal role in guiding their organizations through this process by implementing practical strategies to mitigate risks and address bias in algorithmic systems. In this section, we'll outline practical guidance on how IT leaders can achieve these objectives, including conducting bias audits, sensitivity analyses, implementing fairness-aware algorithms, and utilizing diverse datasets.

1. Conduct Bias Audits:

IT leaders should conduct bias audits to assess the potential biases present in algorithmic systems. Bias audits involve analyzing the inputs, outputs, and decision-making processes of algorithms to identify and quantify biases related to factors such as race, gender, ethnicity, or socioeconomic status. By conducting bias audits, IT leaders can identify areas where bias may exist and develop strategies to mitigate its impact on algorithmic decision-making.

2. Perform Sensitivity Analyses:

Sensitivity analyses involve testing the robustness of algorithmic systems to variations in input data and model parameters. IT leaders should perform sensitivity analyses to understand how changes in input data, preprocessing techniques, or algorithmic parameters affect the outcomes of algorithmic decisions. By conducting sensitivity analyses, IT leaders can identify potential vulnerabilities or weaknesses in algorithmic systems and implement safeguards to mitigate risks.

3. Implement Fairness-Aware Algorithms:

Fairness-aware algorithms are designed to mitigate bias and ensure equitable outcomes for all stakeholders. IT leaders should implement fairness-aware algorithms that incorporate fairness constraints or criteria into the decision-making process. These algorithms can adjust decision outcomes to ensure that they are fair and unbiased across different demographic groups. By implementing fairness-aware algorithms, IT leaders can mitigate the risk of bias and discrimination in algorithmic decision-making.

4. Utilize Diverse Datasets:

Diverse datasets are essential for training algorithms that are robust, reliable, and free from bias. IT leaders should utilize diverse datasets that represent the full range of demographic characteristics, socioeconomic backgrounds, and cultural contexts present in the target population. By using diverse datasets, IT leaders can reduce the risk of bias and ensure that algorithms generalize well to diverse populations. Additionally,

IT leaders should regularly monitor and update datasets to ensure that they remain current, relevant, and representative of the target population.

5. Establish Bias Mitigation Policies and Procedures:

IT leaders should establish bias mitigation policies and procedures to guide the development, deployment, and monitoring of algorithmic systems. These policies and procedures should outline best practices for identifying, mitigating, and addressing bias in algorithmic decision-making processes. Additionally, IT leaders should provide training and resources to stakeholders involved in algorithmic decision-making to raise awareness of bias-related issues and equip them with the skills and knowledge needed to address bias effectively.

Key Takeaways

Mitigating risks and addressing bias in algorithmic decision-making is essential for organizations to ensure fairness, transparency, and ethical integrity. IT leaders should implement practical strategies such as conducting bias audits, performing sensitivity analyses, implementing fairness-aware algorithms, utilizing diverse datasets, and establishing bias mitigation policies and procedures. By taking proactive steps to mitigate risks and address bias, IT leaders can ensure that their organizations' algorithmic systems are fair, transparent, and aligned with ethical standards.

Navigating data ethics is a critical responsibility for IT leaders in the data-driven age. By addressing the ethical challenges associated with algorithmic decision-making and implementing strategies to promote fairness, accountability, and transparency, IT leaders can ensure that their organizations harness the power of data and AI responsibly and ethically.

Chapter V: Building a Data-Driven Culture

In today's digital age, data has emerged as a strategic asset that drives innovation, informs decision-making, and shapes organizational success. Building a data-driven culture is essential for organizations looking to thrive in this rapidly evolving landscape. In this chapter, we will explore strategies for cultivating a data-driven culture, empowering employees to make informed decisions, fostering collaboration between IT and business units, and encouraging experimentation and continuous learning.

A. Cultivating Data Literacy Across the Organization

Data literacy is the foundation of a data-driven culture, empowering employees at all levels to effectively interpret, analyze, and act upon data-driven insights.

In today's data-driven world, cultivating data literacy across the organization is essential for building a culture that values and leverages data to drive informed decision-making and business success. Data literacy refers to the ability of individuals to read, interpret, analyze, and communicate data effectively. In this section, we'll outline the importance of promoting data literacy across the organization, highlighting the benefits of equipping employees with the skills and knowledge they need to make informed decisions based on data.

1. Empowering Informed Decision-Making:

Promoting data literacy empowers employees at all levels of the organization to make informed decisions based on data-driven insights. By equipping employees with the skills to interpret and analyze data, organizations can harness the collective intelligence of their workforce to identify opportunities, solve problems, and drive innovation. Data-literate employees are better equipped to understand complex data sets, extract meaningful insights, and apply data-driven approaches to their decision-making processes.

2. Driving Organizational Performance:

Data literacy is closely linked to organizational performance and competitiveness. Organizations with a strong data-driven culture outperform their peers by leveraging data to optimize processes, identify trends, and make strategic decisions. By promoting data literacy across the organization, organizations can unlock the full potential of their data assets and gain a competitive edge in the marketplace. Data-literate employees are better positioned to identify areas for improvement, optimize workflows, and drive continuous improvement initiatives that enhance organizational performance.

3. Fostering Innovation and Creativity:

Data literacy fosters a culture of innovation and creativity within the organization. When employees have the skills and knowledge to explore and analyze data, they are more likely to identify novel solutions to complex problems and generate innovative ideas that drive business growth. Data-literate employees are better equipped to experiment with new approaches, test hypotheses, and iterate on solutions, leading to the development of new products, services, and processes that differentiate the organization in the marketplace.

4. Enhancing Collaboration and Communication:

Promoting data literacy facilitates collaboration and communication across teams and departments within the organization. When employees share a common understanding of data concepts and methodologies, they can collaborate more effectively on projects, share insights and best practices, and align their efforts toward common goals. Data-literate employees are better able to communicate their findings and insights to stakeholders, facilitating decision-making and driving consensus around data-driven initiatives.

5. Nurturing a Learning Culture:

Promoting data literacy nurtures a culture of continuous learning and development within the organization. As data technologies and methodologies evolve, employees must continually update their skills and knowledge to remain effective in their roles. By providing opportunities for training, education, and skills development in data literacy, organizations can empower employees to stay abreast of emerging trends and technologies and adapt to evolving business needs.

Promoting data literacy across the organization is essential for building a culture that values and leverages data to drive informed decision-making and business success. Data-literate employees are empowered to make informed decisions, drive organizational performance, foster innovation and creativity, enhance collaboration and communication, and nurture a culture of continuous learning and development. By investing in data literacy initiatives, organizations can unlock the full potential of their data assets and position themselves for long-term success in today's data-driven world.

By investing in data literacy initiatives, organizations can empower employees to unlock the full potential of data, driving innovation, and driving organizational success. Whether it's through training programs, workshops, or educational resources, there are various ways that organizations can cultivate data literacy across the organization, ensuring that every employee has the skills they need to thrive in the data-driven age.

B. Fostering Collaboration Between IT and Business Units

Effective collaboration between IT and business units is essential for building a data-driven culture that aligns technological capabilities with strategic objectives.

Fostering collaboration between IT and business units is essential for driving a data-driven culture and achieving organizational success. Collaboration between these two critical functions enables organizations to align technological capabilities with strategic objectives, leverage data to make informed decisions and drive innovation across the organization. In this section, we'll outline the importance of collaboration between IT and business units, highlighting the benefits of aligning technological capabilities with strategic objectives.

1. Aligning Technological Capabilities with Strategic Objectives:

Collaboration between IT and business units ensures that technological capabilities are aligned with strategic objectives. IT teams possess the technical expertise to design, implement, and maintain data infrastructure and systems, while business units understand the organization's goals, challenges, and opportunities. By collaborating closely, IT and business units can identify technological solutions that address business needs and support strategic initiatives, ensuring that technological investments deliver maximum value to the organization.

2. Leveraging Data to Make Informed Decisions:

Collaboration between IT and business units enables organizations to leverage data to make informed decisions. IT teams are responsible for collecting, storing, and analyzing data, while business units have domain expertise and understand the context in which data is used. By working together, IT and business units can identify relevant data sources, develop analytics capabilities, and generate insights that inform strategic decision-making. This collaboration ensures that data-driven insights are aligned with business priorities and contribute to organizational success.

3. Driving Innovation Across the Organization:

Collaboration between IT and business units drives innovation across the organization. IT teams are at the forefront of technological innovation, while business units are best positioned to identify opportunities for innovation within their areas of expertise. By collaborating closely, IT and business units can develop and implement innovative solutions that address business challenges, improve processes, and create new growth opportunities. This collaboration fosters a culture of innovation and enables organizations to stay ahead of the competition in a rapidly changing marketplace.

4. Enhancing Agility and Responsiveness:

Collaboration between IT and business units enhances agility and responsiveness within the organization. In today's dynamic business environment, organizations must be able to adapt quickly to changing market conditions, customer needs, and technological advancements. By collaborating closely, IT and business units can identify emerging trends, anticipate future challenges, and develop agile solutions that enable the organization to respond rapidly to changing circumstances. This collaboration ensures that the organization remains competitive and resilient in the face of uncertainty.

5. Promoting Cross-Functional Understanding and Communication:

Collaboration between IT and business units promotes cross-functional understanding and communication. IT teams and business units often have different perspectives, priorities, and communication styles, which can lead to misunderstandings and misalignment. By fostering collaboration, organizations can bridge the gap between IT and business units, facilitate communication, and foster a shared understanding of goals, challenges, and opportunities. This collaboration fosters a culture of teamwork and collaboration, enabling organizations to achieve their strategic objectives more effectively.

Fostering collaboration between IT and business units is essential for driving a data-driven culture and achieving organizational success. Collaboration enables organizations to align technological capabilities with strategic objectives, leverage data to make informed decisions, drive innovation across the organization, enhance agility and responsiveness, and promote cross-functional understanding and communication. By working together, IT and business units can harness the power of data and technology to drive organizational growth, innovation, and success in today's competitive business landscape.

C. Encouraging Experimentation and Learning from Data

Organizations must embrace a culture of experimentation and continuous learning to stay ahead of the curve.

Leveraging data to drive innovation and organizational growth is essential for staying competitive and relevant. Encouraging experimentation and learning from data enables organizations to unlock new opportunities, identify potential risks, and drive continuous improvement and innovation. By embracing a culture of experimentation and learning, organizations can remain agile, responsive, and innovative in the face of change. In this section, we'll explore the value of leveraging data to drive innovation and organizational growth, highlighting the benefits of encouraging experimentation and learning from data.

1. Unlocking New Opportunities:

Encouraging experimentation and learning from data enables organizations to unlock new opportunities for growth and innovation. By analyzing data from various sources, organizations can identify emerging trends, customer preferences, and market opportunities that may not be apparent through traditional methods. Experimentation allows organizations to test new ideas, products, and business models, enabling them to explore new markets, launch innovative products, and diversify revenue streams.

2. Identifying Potential Risks:

Experimentation and learning from data also help organizations identify potential risks and challenges before they escalate into larger problems. By analyzing data and conducting experiments, organizations can assess the potential impact of different scenarios and make informed decisions to mitigate risks. For example, A/B testing can help organizations evaluate the effectiveness of marketing campaigns or product features before launching them to a wider audience, reducing the risk of failure and minimizing costly mistakes.

3. Driving Continuous Improvement and Innovation:

Experimentation and learning from data drive continuous improvement and innovation within organizations. By analyzing data on an ongoing basis and learning from past experiences, organizations can identify areas for optimization, refine their strategies, and drive incremental performance improvements. This iterative approach to innovation enables organizations to stay ahead of the competition, adapt to changing market conditions, and continuously deliver value to customers.

4. Promoting a Culture of Innovation and Creativity:

Encouraging experimentation and learning from data promotes a culture of innovation and creativity within organizations. By empowering employees to explore new ideas, test hypotheses, and take calculated risks, organizations foster a spirit of innovation that drives business growth and success. Employees feel empowered to challenge the status quo, think outside the box, and develop innovative solutions to complex problems, leading to breakthroughs that propel the organization forward.

5. Embracing Data-Driven Decision-Making:

Experimentation and learning from data promote data-driven decision-making processes within organizations. By basing decisions on empirical evidence and insights derived from data analysis, organizations can make informed choices that drive business results. Data-driven decision-making reduces reliance on intuition and guesswork, enabling organizations to make strategic decisions with confidence and precision.

Key Takeaways

Encouraging experimentation and learning from data is essential for organizations looking to thrive in today's digital age. By leveraging data to drive innovation and organizational growth, organizations can unlock new opportunities, identify potential risks, and drive continuous improvement and innovation. Whether through pilot projects, A/B testing, or data-driven decision-making processes, organizations can cultivate a culture of experimentation and learning that empowers employees, fosters innovation, and drives organizational success.

Chapter VI: Leading Through Change

It's crucial to acknowledge that navigating the waters of organizational transformation requires a steadfast commitment to principles that withstand the test of time. In this chapter, we will explore how leaders can guide their organizations through the adoption of algorithmic solutions, overcoming resistance, managing cultural shifts, and effectively communicating the value of data-driven initiatives.

A. Overcoming Resistance to Algorithmic Adoption

In every organization, resistance to change is an inevitable hurdle that leaders must overcome. When it comes to the adoption of algorithmic solutions, this resistance can manifest in various forms – from skepticism about the technology's efficacy to fear of job displacement.

However, as leaders, we must address these concerns head-on and inspire confidence in the transformative potential of algorithmic solutions.

By fostering a culture of openness and transparency, engaging stakeholders in the decision-making process, and providing ample training and support, leaders can help mitigate resistance and pave the way for successful algorithmic adoption. It's essential to approach resistance with empathy and understanding, acknowledging the legitimate concerns of employees while highlighting the benefits and opportunities that algorithmic solutions bring to the organization.

B. Managing Cultural Shifts and Organizational Dynamics

Algorithmic adoption isn't just about implementing new technology – it's about fundamentally reshaping the way we work and interact within our organizations. This shift in culture and dynamics can be both exhilarating and daunting, requiring leaders to navigate uncharted waters with clarity and purpose.

The adoption of algorithms within an organization necessitates significant cultural shifts and organizational dynamics. These changes can disrupt established workflows, challenge traditional hierarchies, and require employees to adapt to new ways of working. Effectively managing these cultural shifts is essential for ensuring successful algorithmic adoption and maximizing the benefits of data-driven decision-making. In this section, we'll explore the cultural shifts and organizational dynamics that accompany algorithmic adoption and offer insights into effective change management strategies.

1. Understanding Cultural Shifts:

Algorithmic adoption often requires a shift in organizational culture towards one that values data-driven decision-making, collaboration, and innovation. This may involve challenging existing beliefs and practices, fostering a greater openness to experimentation and risk-taking, and promoting a culture of learning and adaptability. Understanding the cultural shifts that accompany algorithmic adoption is essential for leaders to effectively navigate change and foster a supportive environment for innovation and growth.

2. Recognizing Organizational Dynamics:

Algorithmic adoption can also impact organizational dynamics, including power structures, communication channels, and decision-making processes. As algorithms become integral to decision-making, traditional hierarchies may become less relevant, and cross-functional collaboration may become more important. Leaders must recognize these shifts in organizational dynamics and adapt their leadership style and organizational structures accordingly to foster collaboration, trust, and innovation.

3. Change Management Strategies:

Effective change management is crucial for managing cultural shifts and organizational dynamics in algorithmic adoption. Leaders should communicate transparently with employees about the reasons for adopting algorithms, the expected benefits, and how it will impact their roles and responsibilities. Additionally, leaders should provide training and support to help employees develop the skills and knowledge needed to work with algorithms effectively. Creating opportunities for collaboration, feedback, and participation in decision-making processes can also help to build buy-in and foster a sense of ownership and commitment to change.

4. Fostering a Culture of Collaboration, Trust, and Innovation:

Leaders play a critical role in fostering a culture of collaboration, trust, and innovation that supports algorithmic adoption. By modeling the behaviors and values that support a culture of continuous improvement and growth, leaders can create an environment where employees feel empowered to embrace change and adapt to new ways of working. This may involve encouraging experimentation, recognizing, and rewarding innovative ideas, and creating channels for open communication and knowledge sharing.

5. Leading by Example:

Leading by example is essential for driving cultural shifts and organizational dynamics in algorithmic adoption. Leaders should demonstrate a commitment to data-driven decision-making, collaboration, and innovation in their actions and decisions. By embodying the values and behaviors that support algorithmic adoption, leaders can inspire confidence and trust in employees and create a positive organizational culture that embraces change and drives business success.

C. Communicating the Value of Data-Driven Initiatives

Effective communication is the lifeblood of successful organizational change. As leaders, it's our responsibility to articulate the value proposition of data-driven initiatives in a way that resonates with stakeholders at all levels of the organization. Whether it's demonstrating the tangible benefits of algorithmic solutions through real-world examples or highlighting the opportunities for innovation and growth, effective communication is key to gaining buy-in and driving organizational change.

Effective communication is essential for gaining buy-in and mobilizing support for data-driven initiatives within an organization. By clearly and authentically communicating the value of these initiatives, leaders can inspire confidence, build trust, and foster a culture of innovation and collaboration. In this section, we'll discuss strategies for effectively communicating the value of data-driven initiatives, emphasizing the importance of clarity, consistency, and authenticity.

1. Tailoring Communication to the Audience:

One of the most critical aspects of effective communication is tailoring the message to the needs and preferences of the audience. Different stakeholders within the organization may have varying levels of familiarity with data-driven concepts and varying concerns or priorities. Leaders should adapt their communication approach accordingly, using language and examples that resonate with the audience and address their specific interests and concerns.

2. Emphasizing Clarity and Consistency:

Clarity and consistency are essential for ensuring that the message is understood and retained by the audience. Leaders should communicate the value of data-driven initiatives in clear, straightforward language, avoiding jargon and technical terms that may be unfamiliar to non-technical stakeholders. Additionally, consistency in messaging helps to reinforce key points and build trust over time, ensuring that the organization remains aligned and focused on its goals.

3. Providing Concrete Examples and Case Studies:

Concrete examples and case studies are powerful tools for illustrating the value of data-driven initiatives in real-world contexts. Leaders should provide tangible examples of how data-driven approaches have led to positive outcomes, such as improved decision-making, increased efficiency, or enhanced customer experiences. These examples help to make the benefits of data-driven initiatives more tangible and relatable to stakeholders, increasing buy-in and support.

4. Engaging Stakeholders in Two-Way Communication:

Effective communication is not just about delivering messages; it's also about listening to stakeholders and engaging them in two-way communication. Leaders should create opportunities for dialogue and feedback, allowing stakeholders to ask questions, share concerns, and provide input on data-driven initiatives. By involving stakeholders in the communication process, leaders can build trust, foster a sense of ownership, and ensure that the needs and perspectives of all stakeholders are considered.

5. Demonstrating Authenticity and Transparency:

Authenticity and transparency are essential for building trust and credibility with stakeholders. Leaders should communicate openly and honestly about the opportunities and challenges associated with data-driven initiatives, acknowledging any uncertainties or risks. By demonstrating authenticity and transparency, leaders can foster a culture of trust and accountability within the organization, inspiring confidence in data-driven decision-making processes.

Key Takeaways

Effective communication is essential for gaining buy-in and mobilizing support for data-driven initiatives within an organization. By tailoring communication to the needs and preferences of the audience, emphasizing clarity, consistency, and authenticity, and engaging stakeholders in two-way communication, leaders can build trust, inspire confidence, and mobilize support for algorithmic adoption across the organization. Leading through change requires a combination of vision, empathy, and effective communication, and by overcoming resistance, managing cultural shifts, and articulating the value of data-driven initiatives, leaders can guide their organizations to success in today's data-driven world.

Chapter VII: Case Studies and Practical Examples

In this chapter, we will delve into real-world case studies and practical examples that illustrate the implementation of algorithmic solutions in various industries. From successful implementations to lessons learned from failures and challenges, these case studies provide valuable insights and actionable takeaways for IT leaders looking to leverage algorithms effectively within their organizations.

A. Real-world Examples of Successful Algorithmic Implementations

Let's begin by exploring real-world examples of successful algorithmic implementations that have driven tangible results and transformed organizations. From predictive analytics in healthcare to optimization algorithms in logistics, these case studies showcase how algorithmic solutions can unlock new opportunities, drive innovation, and create value for stakeholders.

In recent years, organizations across various industries have leveraged algorithmic solutions to drive tangible results, transform operations, and create value for stakeholders. These real-world examples highlight the power of algorithmic implementations in unlocking new opportunities, driving innovation, and delivering impactful outcomes.

Let's explore some of these case studies:

1. Predictive Analytics in Healthcare:

Healthcare organizations have increasingly turned to predictive analytics to improve patient outcomes, optimize resource allocation, and reduce costs. For example, a major national hospital implemented a predictive analytics model to identify patients at high risk of readmission within 30 days of discharge. By analyzing patient data, including demographic information, medical history, and previous hospitalizations, the model accurately predicted readmission risk, allowing clinicians to intervene proactively and provide targeted interventions to prevent readmissions. This algorithmic solution not only improved patient outcomes but also reduced healthcare costs by minimizing unnecessary hospitalizations.

2. Optimization Algorithms in Logistics:

Logistics companies have embraced optimization algorithms to streamline operations, optimize routes, and reduce transportation costs. One notable example is a large delivery service, which developed its own proprietary routing algorithm. The algorithm analyzes vast amounts of data, including package volume, delivery constraints, and traffic patterns, to generate optimized delivery routes for drivers. By minimizing the distance traveled and maximizing delivery efficiency, the algorithm has enabled delivery service to reduce fuel consumption, lower operating costs, and enhance customer satisfaction.

3. Personalized Recommendations in E-Commerce:

E-commerce platforms utilize recommendation algorithms to personalize the shopping experience and drive sales. Amazon, for instance, employs sophisticated recommendation algorithms that analyze customer browsing behavior, purchase history, and demographic information to generate personalized product recommendations. By presenting relevant products to shoppers based on their preferences and interests, Amazon increases engagement, encourages repeat purchases, and boosts revenue. These recommendation algorithms have become integral to Amazon's success and have set a precedent for personalized shopping experiences in the e-commerce industry.

4. Fraud Detection in Finance:

Financial institutions rely on fraud detection algorithms to identify and prevent fraudulent activities, safeguarding against financial losses and protecting customer assets. PayPal, for example, employs machine learning algorithms to analyze transaction data in real-time and detect suspicious patterns indicative of fraudulent behavior. By flagging potentially fraudulent transactions for further review, PayPal can mitigate risk and prevent unauthorized transactions, enhancing security and instilling trust among users.

5. Dynamic Pricing in Hospitality:

Hospitality companies leverage dynamic pricing algorithms to optimize pricing strategies, maximize revenue, and improve profitability. Hotels and airlines, for instance, use revenue management algorithms to adjust prices in real-time based on factors such as demand, occupancy rates, and competitor pricing. By dynamically adjusting prices to reflect market conditions and demand fluctuations, hospitality companies can capture additional revenue opportunities, increase yield, and improve overall financial performance.

These real-world examples demonstrate the transformative impact of algorithmic implementations across various industries. From predictive analytics in healthcare to optimization algorithms in logistics, algorithmic solutions have driven tangible results, unlocked new opportunities, and created value for stakeholders. By harnessing the power of algorithms, organizations can innovate, optimize operations, and stay competitive in today's data-driven world.

Best Practices and Lessons Learned

Industry leaders have demonstrated a variety of strategies and approaches that have contributed to the success of algorithmic implementations in their organizations. By studying these examples, IT leaders can gain valuable insights into how to effectively leverage algorithms within their organizations and drive meaningful results.

Let's explore some of the best practices and lessons learned from industry leaders:

1. Data Quality and Preparation:

Industry leaders prioritize data quality and invest in data preparation processes to ensure that algorithms are trained on clean, reliable data. They understand that the quality of input data directly impacts the accuracy and effectiveness of algorithmic solutions.

2. Cross-Functional Collaboration:

Successful algorithmic implementations involve collaboration between IT teams, data scientists, business analysts, and other stakeholders. Industry leaders recognize the importance of cross-functional collaboration in aligning algorithmic solutions with strategic objectives and ensuring that they meet the needs of end-users.

3. Agile Development and Iterative Testing:

Agile development methodologies and iterative testing are key to the success of algorithmic implementations. Industry leaders embrace an iterative approach to development, allowing them to quickly prototype, test, and refine algorithms based on feedback and real-world performance.

4. Ethical Considerations and Bias Mitigation:

Ethical considerations and bias mitigation are paramount in algorithmic implementations. Industry leaders prioritize fairness, accountability, and transparency in their algorithms and implement measures to mitigate biases and ensure ethical decision-making.

5. Scalability and Performance Optimization:

Scalability and performance optimization are critical considerations in algorithmic implementations, especially in large-scale deployments. Industry leaders design algorithms with scalability in mind, ensuring that they can handle increasing volumes of data and maintain optimal performance under various conditions.

6. Continuous Learning and Improvement:

Industry leaders embrace a culture of continuous learning and improvement, recognizing that the landscape of algorithms and data science is constantly evolving. They invest in ongoing training and development for their teams and prioritize staying abreast of emerging trends and technologies in the field.

7. Customer-Centric Approach:

A customer-centric approach is central to the success of algorithmic implementations. Industry leaders focus on understanding customer needs and preferences and use algorithms to deliver personalized experiences, tailored recommendations, and value-added services that enhance customer satisfaction and loyalty.

8. Change Management and Communication:

Change management and effective communication are essential for driving adoption and ensuring the success of algorithmic implementations. Industry leaders communicate transparently with stakeholders about the rationale for algorithmic solutions, the expected benefits, and how they will impact workflows and processes.

9. Regulatory Compliance and Governance:

Regulatory compliance and governance are top priorities for industry leaders implementing algorithmic solutions, particularly in highly regulated industries such as healthcare and finance. They ensure that algorithms comply with relevant regulations and adhere to industry standards for data privacy, security, and ethics.

10. Measurement and Monitoring:

Measurement and monitoring are key components of successful algorithmic implementations. Industry leaders establish KPIs and performance metrics to track the effectiveness and impact of algorithms over time, allowing them to identify areas for improvement and optimize outcomes.

Best practices and lessons learned from industry leaders offer valuable guidance for IT leaders looking to effectively leverage algorithms within their organizations. By prioritizing data quality, fostering cross-functional collaboration, embracing agile development, addressing ethical considerations, and adopting a customer-centric approach, IT leaders can drive successful algorithmic implementations and deliver tangible value to their organizations and stakeholders.

B. Lessons Learned from Failures and Challenges

Not every algorithmic implementation is a success story, and it's essential to learn from failures and challenges to avoid repeating the same mistakes.

Failed algorithmic implementations offer valuable insights into the common pitfalls and challenges that organizations encounter along the way. From issues of data quality and model accuracy to challenges in organizational readiness and change management, understanding these lessons learned can help IT leaders better prepare for the implementation of algorithmic solutions and increase the likelihood of success. Let's explore some of the key lessons learned from failures and challenges in algorithmic initiatives:

1. Data Quality and Accuracy:

One of the most common challenges in algorithmic implementations is poor data quality and accuracy. Organizations may encounter issues such as incomplete or inconsistent data, biased datasets, or inaccuracies in data collection methods. Without clean, reliable data, algorithms may produce inaccurate or misleading results, leading to suboptimal decision-making and failed initiatives.

2. Lack of Organizational Readiness:

Another challenge is a lack of organizational readiness for algorithmic adoption. Organizations may not have the necessary infrastructure, resources, or expertise in place to support algorithmic initiatives. Additionally, cultural resistance or skepticism towards data-driven approaches can hinder adoption and implementation efforts, leading to resistance and pushback from employees.

3. Overlooking Ethical Considerations:

Ethical considerations are often overlooked in algorithmic implementations, leading to unintended consequences and ethical dilemmas. Organizations may inadvertently perpetuate biases or discrimination through algorithmic decision-making, resulting in unfair outcomes or harm to vulnerable populations. Failing to address ethical considerations can damage trust and credibility, leading to backlash and reputational damage.

4. Insufficient Change Management:

Change management is essential for the successful adoption and implementation of algorithmic solutions. Organizations may struggle to effectively communicate the rationale for algorithmic initiatives, engage stakeholders, and manage resistance to change. Without a proactive approach to change management, organizations risk encountering roadblocks and delays in implementation efforts.

5. Complexity and Overengineering:

Overly complex algorithms or overengineering solutions can pose significant challenges in implementation and maintenance. Organizations may attempt to develop overly sophisticated algorithms without considering practicality or scalability, leading to unnecessary complexity and resource constraints. Simplifying algorithms and focusing on practical, achievable goals can help mitigate these challenges and improve implementation outcomes.

6. Lack of Monitoring and Feedback Loops:

Failing to establish monitoring mechanisms and feedback loops can hinder the success of algorithmic implementations. Organizations may overlook the importance of ongoing performance evaluation and fail to iterate or refine algorithms based on feedback and real-world performance. Establishing robust monitoring and evaluation processes allows organizations to identify issues early, make necessary adjustments, and optimize outcomes over time.

7. Regulatory and Compliance Risks:

Regulatory and compliance risks can pose significant challenges in algorithmic implementations, particularly in highly regulated industries such as healthcare and finance. Organizations may fail to adequately address legal and regulatory requirements, leading to compliance issues, fines, or legal liabilities. Prioritizing regulatory compliance and establishing robust governance frameworks are essential for mitigating these risks and ensuring the ethical, legal, and responsible use of algorithms.

Lessons learned from failures and challenges in algorithmic implementations highlight the importance of addressing issues such as data quality, organizational readiness, ethical considerations, change management, complexity, monitoring, and regulatory compliance. By understanding these challenges and learning from the experiences of others, IT leaders can better prepare for the implementation of algorithmic solutions and increase the likelihood of success. Taking a proactive approach to addressing these challenges and prioritizing ethical, responsible, and transparent use of algorithms is essential for driving positive outcomes and maximizing the benefits of data-driven decision-making within organizations.

C. Practical Insights for IT Leaders

Drawing from the case studies and examples discussed in the previous sections, IT leaders can distill practical insights and actionable takeaways to effectively leverage algorithms within their organizations. These insights encompass key learnings and best practices that IT leaders can apply to drive successful algorithmic implementations and unlock the full potential of data-driven decision-making. Let's explore some of these practical insights:

1. Establish a Strong Foundation of Data Governance:

Prioritize data governance to ensure that data is accurate, reliable, and secure. Implement robust data management practices, including data quality assurance, data privacy protection, and compliance with regulatory requirements. By establishing a strong foundation of data governance, IT leaders can lay the groundwork for successful algorithmic implementations and mitigate risks associated with poor data quality or compliance issues.

2. Foster a Culture of Experimentation and Learning:

Encourage a culture of experimentation and continuous learning within the organization. Create opportunities for employees to explore new ideas, test hypotheses, and develop innovative solutions using algorithms. Embrace a growth mindset that values learning from failures and iterating on ideas to drive continuous improvement. By fostering a culture of experimentation and learning, IT leaders can empower their teams to innovate and drive organizational success.

3. Communicate the Value of Algorithmic Initiatives Effectively:

Effectively communicate the value of algorithmic initiatives to stakeholders across the organization. Tailor communication strategies to address the specific needs and preferences of different audiences, using clear, concise language and relatable examples to illustrate the benefits of data-driven decision-making. Emphasize the potential impact on key business metrics such as cost savings, revenue growth, and customer satisfaction to gain buy-in and support from stakeholders.

4. Prioritize Ethical Considerations and Bias Mitigation:

Prioritize ethical considerations and bias mitigation throughout the algorithmic implementation process. Conduct thorough ethical assessments to identify potential biases or ethical dilemmas in algorithmic decision-making. Implement fairness-aware algorithms, diversity in datasets, and transparency measures to mitigate biases and ensure ethical outcomes. By prioritizing ethics and accountability, IT leaders can build trust and credibility in algorithmic solutions and protect against unintended consequences.

5. Embrace Agile Development and Iterative Testing:

Embrace agile development methodologies and iterative testing to accelerate the implementation and refinement of algorithmic solutions. Break down projects into smaller, manageable tasks and iterate on algorithms based on feedback and real-world performance. Adopt a flexible approach that allows for rapid prototyping, experimentation, and adaptation to changing requirements or conditions. By embracing agility and iteration, IT leaders can expedite the development process and deliver value to the organization more quickly.

6. Invest in Talent Development and Collaboration:

Invest in talent development and collaboration to build a diverse team with the skills and expertise needed to implement and optimize algorithmic solutions. Foster collaboration between IT teams, data scientists, business analysts, and other stakeholders to leverage collective knowledge and expertise. Provide opportunities for training, mentorship, and professional development to ensure that team members stay abreast of emerging trends and technologies in the field. By investing in talent development and collaboration, IT leaders can build a high-performing team capable of driving successful algorithmic implementations.

Key Takeaways

IT leaders can leverage practical insights and actionable takeaways to drive successful algorithmic implementations within their organizations. By establishing a strong foundation of data governance, fostering a culture of experimentation and learning, effectively communicating the value of algorithmic initiatives, prioritizing ethical considerations and bias mitigation, embracing agile development and iterative testing, and investing in talent development and collaboration,

IT leaders can unlock the full potential of algorithms and drive organizational success in today's data-driven world. The case studies and practical examples presented in this chapter provide valuable insights and guidance for IT leaders embarking on the journey of algorithmic implementation. By learning from both the successes and failures of others, IT leaders can increase their chances of success and drive meaningful results within their organizations.

Chapter VIII: The Future of IT Leadership

As we gaze into the horizon of technological advancement, it becomes evident that the future of IT leadership is intricately intertwined with the evolution of data and artificial intelligence. In this chapter, we will explore emerging trends in data and AI, discuss how IT leaders can adapt their leadership practices to keep pace with technological advancements and emphasize the importance of continuous improvement in the pursuit of algorithmic excellence.

A. Anticipating Trends in Data and AI

The landscape of data and artificial intelligence is constantly evolving, with new trends and technologies emerging at a rapid pace. As technology continues to evolve at a rapid pace, IT leaders must anticipate key trends shaping the future of data and artificial intelligence (AI). By staying ahead of these trends, IT leaders can position their organizations for success in an increasingly data-driven world.

Let's explore some of the key trends shaping the future of data and AI:

1. Rise of Edge Computing:

Edge computing involves processing data closer to its source, reducing latency, and enabling real-time decision-making. With the proliferation of Internet of Things (IoT) devices and the increasing volume of data generated at the edge, edge computing is poised to become a critical component of IT infrastructure. IT leaders should anticipate the need to invest in edge computing technologies and develop strategies for managing and analyzing data at the edge to unlock new opportunities for innovation and efficiency.

2. Federated Learning and Privacy-Preserving AI:

Federated learning allows for decentralized model training across multiple devices or edge nodes without sharing raw data, preserving user privacy. As privacy concerns continue to grow and regulations such as GDPR and CCPA become more stringent, federated learning offers a promising approach to AI model training while protecting sensitive user data. IT leaders should explore the potential applications of federated learning in their organizations and invest in technologies that enable privacy-preserving AI to maintain compliance and build trust with customers.

3. Integration of AI into Everyday Devices and Applications:

AI is increasingly being integrated into everyday devices and applications, ranging from smartphones and wearables to smart home devices and industrial equipment. This trend, often referred to as embedded AI or AI at the edge, enables intelligent functionality and automation in a wide range of contexts. IT leaders should anticipate the growing demand for AI-enabled products and services and explore opportunities to integrate AI into their organization's offerings to enhance customer experiences, improve operational efficiency, and drive innovation.

4. Augmented Analytics and Explainable AI:

Augmented analytics leverages AI and machine learning algorithms to automate data preparation, analysis, and insight generation, empowering business users to make data-driven decisions more effectively. Explainable AI focuses on making AI models more transparent and understandable, enabling users to interpret and trust AI-driven recommendations and decisions. IT leaders should prioritize investments in augmented analytics and explainable AI tools to democratize data access and promote data-driven decision-making across the organization.

5. Ethical AI and Responsible Innovation:

As AI becomes more pervasive in society, ensuring ethical AI and responsible innovation are critical priorities for IT leaders. Organizations must address concerns related to bias, fairness, transparency, and accountability in AI systems to build trust and mitigate risks. IT leaders should develop policies, processes, and governance frameworks to guide the ethical use of AI within their organizations and actively engage with stakeholders to foster a culture of responsible innovation and AI literacy.

6. Quantum Computing and Advanced AI Algorithms:

Quantum computing holds the potential to revolutionize AI by enabling the development of more powerful algorithms capable of solving complex problems at scale. While quantum computing is still in its early stages, IT leaders should monitor advancements in this field and explore potential applications for quantum AI in their organizations. Additionally, advancements in advanced AI algorithms, such as deep learning, reinforcement learning, and generative models, offer opportunities to tackle increasingly complex challenges and drive innovation in AI-driven solutions.

IT leaders must anticipate key trends in data and AI to effectively lead their organizations in an increasingly data-driven world. By staying ahead of trends such as the rise of edge computing, federated learning, integration of AI into everyday devices, augmented analytics, ethical AI, and quantum computing, IT leaders can capitalize on opportunities for innovation, drive strategic investments in emerging technologies, and create value for their organizations and stakeholders.

B. Adapting Leadership Practices to Technological Advancements

As technology continues to advance at an unprecedented pace, IT leaders must adapt their leadership practices to keep pace with change.

IT leaders must cultivate agility, resilience, and adaptability to ensure they remain responsive to evolving needs and challenges. Here's how IT leaders can adapt their leadership practices to navigate the changing technological landscape:

1. Embrace a Growth Mindset:

Embrace a growth mindset that views challenges as opportunities for learning and growth. Encourage curiosity, experimentation, and continuous learning among team members. By fostering a growth mindset, IT leaders can create a culture that embraces change and innovation, enabling teams to adapt more effectively to technological advancements.

2. Foster a Culture of Innovation:

Foster a culture of innovation where creativity and experimentation are encouraged. Provide employees with the autonomy and resources they need to explore new ideas and technologies. Celebrate and recognize innovative initiatives, regardless of their outcome, to reinforce a culture that values experimentation and learning.

3. Promote Cross-Functional Collaboration:

Promote cross-functional collaboration by breaking down silos and encouraging communication and collaboration across departments and teams. Facilitate interdisciplinary projects and initiatives that bring together diverse perspectives and expertise. By promoting collaboration, IT leaders can leverage the collective knowledge and skills of their teams to tackle complex technological challenges more effectively.

4. Empower Employees to Take Risks:

Empower employees to take calculated risks and challenge the status quo. Create a safe environment where failure is viewed as a learning opportunity rather than a setback. Encourage employees to experiment with new technologies and approaches, providing support and guidance as needed. By empowering employees to take risks, IT leaders can foster innovation and drive continuous improvement within their organizations.

5. Lead by Example:

Lead by example and demonstrate a willingness to embrace change and adopt new technologies. Stay informed about emerging trends and technologies in the industry and encourage team members to do the same. Be open to feedback and ideas from others and be willing to adapt your leadership style and practices as needed to meet the evolving needs of your team and organization.

6. Develop Adaptive Leadership Skills:

Develop adaptive leadership skills that enable you to navigate uncertainty and complexity effectively. Practice flexibility, resilience, and emotional intelligence in your leadership approach. Be willing to pivot and adjust strategies in response to changing circumstances and demonstrate confidence and composure in the face of adversity. By developing adaptive leadership skills, IT leaders can inspire confidence and trust in their teams and effectively lead them through periods of technological change.

IT leaders must adapt their leadership practices to navigate the ever-changing technological landscape effectively. By embracing a growth mindset, fostering a culture of innovation, promoting cross-functional collaboration, empowering employees to take risks, leading by example, and developing adaptive leadership skills, IT leaders can cultivate agility, resilience, and adaptability in themselves and their teams, ensuring they remain responsive to evolving needs and challenges in the digital age.

C. Continuing the Journey Towards Algorithmic Excellence

Finally, we must emphasize the importance of continuous improvement and learning in the pursuit of algorithmic excellence. In a world where data is abundant and algorithms are ubiquitous, IT leaders must remain committed to refining their skills, processes, and technologies to stay ahead of the curve.

By fostering a culture of continuous improvement and learning, IT leaders can empower their teams to embrace change, experiment with new technologies, and drive innovation. Whether it's through investing in training and development programs, encouraging knowledge sharing and collaboration, or fostering a spirit of curiosity and exploration, there are numerous ways that IT leaders can support their teams on the journey toward algorithmic excellence.

The future of IT leadership is bright and full of possibilities. By anticipating trends in data and AI, adapting leadership practices to technological advancements, and continuing the journey toward algorithmic excellence, IT leaders can position their organizations for success in an increasingly digital and data-driven world.

Chapter IX: Conclusion

As we conclude our journey through the intricacies of IT leadership in a data-driven world, it's essential to reflect on the key insights and takeaways that have emerged from our exploration. In this final chapter, we'll recap the key insights, offer reflections on navigating IT leadership in a data-driven world, and issue a call to action for embracing the algorithmic mindset.

A. Recap of Key Insights

Throughout this book, we've delved into the complexities of IT leadership in the era of big data and artificial intelligence. We've explored the transformative potential of algorithms in driving innovation, the ethical considerations that accompany algorithmic decision-making, and the practical strategies for building a data-driven culture within organizations.

Key insights include the importance of:

- Understanding algorithms and their role in IT leadership.
- Promoting fairness, accountability, and transparency in algorithmic processes.
- Cultivating a data-driven culture through collaboration, experimentation, and learning.
- Navigating resistance and challenges in algorithmic adoption.
- Anticipating trends in data and AI to stay ahead of the curve.

B. Final Thoughts on Navigating IT Leadership in a Data-Driven World

As we look ahead to the future of IT leadership, it's clear that the opportunities presented by data and AI are vast and profound. However, navigating this landscape requires a strategic approach, a commitment to ethical principles, and a willingness to embrace change.

In a data-driven world, IT leaders must be agile, adaptable, and forward-thinking. They must cultivate a culture of innovation, foster collaboration between IT and business units, and continuously seek out new opportunities for leveraging data and algorithms to drive organizational success.

While the road ahead may be challenging, it is also filled with immense potential. By embracing the algorithmic mindset and staying true to the principles of ethical leadership, IT leaders can lead their organizations toward a future of innovation, growth, and prosperity.

C. Call to Action: Embracing the Algorithmic Mindset

As we conclude our journey, I issue a call to action for all readers: embrace the algorithmic mindset. It is not enough to simply understand the principles of data and AI – we must actively apply them in our organizations, driving meaningful change and unlocking new opportunities for innovation.

Whether you're a seasoned IT leader or an aspiring tech professional, now is the time to take proactive steps toward leveraging algorithms effectively within your organization. Embrace a culture of experimentation and learning, advocate for fairness and transparency in algorithmic processes, and lead with integrity and vision.

Together, we can harness the power of data and artificial intelligence to drive positive change, transform our organizations, and shape a brighter future for all. The journey towards algorithmic excellence begins now – let us embark on it together.

www.ingramcontent.com/pod-product-compliance
Lightning Source LLC
Chambersburg PA
CBHW060433290526
45791CB00002B/942